DEDICATION

To my children, Nicholas J. Baca and Emma E. Baca, who remain behind the veil. May you one day know your truth and live by it.

To my children, Loren and Ehren, who saved my life and continue to shine their light on me each day.

To August and Jenny Baca, my parents, whose gifts and talents become more clear the longer I am a parent.

To my brothers, Joel and Mark Baca, thank you for all the big things, and the little ones too.

To Patricia Miller and Geri Saunders, poets who bare witness, and help me speak my truth.

To Kahjarime Baca, T. Lynn Baker, Charles Bernaert, Bonnie J. Boucher, Ray M. Boucher, Kelly Gatlin, David Gonzales, Sam Griego, Bill Houston and Elaine Stewart, who have given me more than friendship.

To Charles Bernaert, Bhanu Harrison, Kevin Rexroad, Nina Ross, Robert Sapien, Stephen Weiss and Bonita Wickstrom, therapists and doctors whose expertise and skill helped to keep me on the path.

To Kay Bounkeua, Loren M. Baca, Bonnie J. Boucher, Ray M. Boucher and Ehren D. Baca for their insights, encouragement and editorial assistance.

To Ray M. Boucher, Ehren D. Baca and Bonnie J. Boucher for their work in designing and creating the cover of this book.

To you, the reader, without whom there would be no story to tell, and no art.

To my friends at Create Space for their help and encouragement.

To my spiritual family, brothers, sisters, parents, children, friends and enemies, given to me in the beginning. You follow me through time, and together we burn our karma.

To Karma, my oldest and unwavering companion.

PROLOGUE

ON BURNING KARMA

Every soul earns its way onto the earth. It may not seem so at times, but it is a necessary privilege to be here. We are all on a mission, a quest if you will. The earth, this space we call the world, is like a cosmic amusement park. It contains surprises, extremes of loss and pain, as well as an abundance of joy and peace. As with an amusement park, you need a pass to get in.

That pass is your karma. It tells you where you have been, suggests what you may do next, and how long to stay. The "where you have been" part of your karma carries with it spiritual, emotional and physical momentum. It is what you have been thinking and doing in the past that continues to link your life with those of other people in the present.

Imagine karma as a sweater that you knitted sometime in the past. You are wearing it now but the yarn-ends extend back into time. As you move forward burning karma, the sweater will pull apart revealing who you really are underneath. The amazing thing about the karmic pass is that it is constantly changing, right before your eyes. It is the original living document.

Take a look at your pass. You will notice that it is a record of where you have been, and a suggestion of where you might go. It is a map that guides you. Here is the beauty, wonder, and the incredibly powerful potential that is your karma. It is only a suggestion. It is written in pencil.

Along with your pass you have also been given a pencil and an eraser. You are free to rewrite your itinerary as you travel through life's journey.

Human beings experience the process of life and the world around them through perception and sensation. Sensations may be physical and or emotional. Sensations are experienced in various levels of intensity.

Karmic sensation originates first as confusion. Confusion is that little annoying tickle you feel in your body when things do not result as you anticipated. Or when you discover that things are not exactly the way you left them. These situations produce confusion because there is an initial lack of connection between the cause in the past, and its effect in the present. When experienced compulsively, even pleasant sensations may produce the sensation of confusion.

With confusion, you have reached the first karmic crossroad. Do not miss this opportunity to stop and notice the gift you have been given. Confusion is not a prelude to disaster it is a wake-up call. It is your karmic compass signaling the first deviation from your perfect journey. If you stop and treat the sensation of confusion with attention and curiosity, you may understand why you are feeling confused, and change your path.

Your karma will always suggest a path that is a product of your past thoughts and actions. If your past thoughts and actions lead to turmoil, your karmic pass will suggest a situation that will feel unsafe or disruptive. If you do not take the time to examine what is happening, and change course, you will not burn your karma. If you continue to react to old situations in the same old ways you will begin to experience pain.

Pain is simply a sensation of discomfort. It may be physical and/or emotional. Pain comes in various intensities. Pain is the second karmic crossroad you will experience if you have not changed your path. At this point you have the option to stop, reassess your life and motivations, change course, and deescalate back to confusion.

It is important to differentiate pain from suffering. Suffering is the inability to deal with pain. In the process of living, death is inevitable, but suffering is always optional. With suffering, you still have the pain. However, now you have compounded it by compulsively spreading it over time. You have begun projecting the specifics of your current pain back into the past, and or forward into the future. Suffering is the third karmic crossroad you will experience. If you suffer long enough and hard enough, you may resort to addiction as a way to find relief.

Addiction is any perception and its resulting sensations and compensations that you feel you cannot stop repeating. Addictive behaviors are chosen. Because they are chosen, you can also un-choose them or break them. The insidious thing about addictions is that initially, they serve a purpose. Briefly, they provide emotional and or physical relief from some situation or behavior that is painful.

Addiction is the end of the line, the darkest corner you will reach. You may have multiple addictions, but there is nothing that comes after addiction. If you are addicted, you may think that you are permanently lost. It may feel that way, but no, you still have your karmic compass. It works perfectly all the time. However you have to be able to look at it and recognize its value. Addiction may make this option seem impossible. It is not impossible, only difficult. Recognize the fact that returning to your ideal journey becomes more and more difficult every time you ignore your karmic compass. This is why it is best to stop and reexamine your path and motivations when you first feel confused.

If we do not stop and take the time to check our karmic pass at the first sign of confusion, we will find ourselves on a very slippery slope. The unpleasant sensation of confusion will escalate to pain, pain to suffering, and suffering to addiction in an endless cycle.

This amusement park we call the world is quite a place indeed. Your karma, the pass you hold, allows you to enter and be welcome anywhere you choose to go. Imagine that! If it is pleasure you desire, or pain, the world holds both in endless variety. Which have you chosen this time?

If you have been in the park for very long, you have probably begun to notice something. Sensations of pleasure or pain come and go. In fact, all emotions and sensations are temporary. If you are addicted, this may not seem so because addictive compensating behaviors are usually chosen within a very narrow gap in time while one is in pain. This is why addictions are hard to break. When the pain we experience is great, we may believe that it is easier to choose some sort of quick relief instead of a change in course. As you walk through the park, these specters of pain and pleasure beckon to you from every side with their promises of relief or gratification. Like carnival workers hawking their attractions, they entice you with the falsehood of sensational delights.

Living in the world is a game of attention and inattention, of spy-verses-spy and counter espionage. We humans are strongly bound to our egos, and as such, we must constantly weigh and measure our motivations and responses. As we make our choices, we are either reinforcing old karma, or burning it.

Years ago I saw a bumper sticker that said, "Shoot your television." The list could now be expanded to shoot your cell phone, pager, movies, billboards, newspapers, magazines, etc. I do not believe that any of these things are evil or intrinsically bad. I do believe that we can make choices concerning where we place our attention. Where we place our attention must include our sensations and thoughts as well. It is the world's job to barrage us with more and more reasons to hunger for extremes of sensation. It is our job to filter out what is best for us and discard the rest. We must become connoisseurs of stimuli. Once we become astute enough to not be endlessly swayed by the sensational hors d'oeuvres being served, we can take a breath and start to enjoy the party that is life.

A pause in the action is the first counterpoint to the confusion you have been feeling. Just imagine what life would be like if you never felt confused. If you were able to stop, make a choice, change your direction and feel better. The world is marvelously benign and impartial. It is not life and the world we eventually succumb to; it is our appetites and the choices we make.

Stop and check your pass. Where does it say you have been? Where does it say you are scheduled to visit? Although it is too late to change where you have been, do not let the lessons you have learned there be wasted. Develop an appreciation for who you have become and the gifts you have been given.

I like to think that karma, the pass and the concept, is a force that you can channel. It is a compass, a passport, a map, a boarding pass, and spending money, all rolled into one. Think of it as a dissolver of confusion and an enabler of your power. It is a leveler of pain and pleasure- a destroyer of addiction.

ON ART AND WRITING

I believe that art is a verb, not a noun. Art is a process of communication. Art is the most elemental, unadulterated and sublime experience that a human being can have. Art is a sensory experience, not an intellectual experience. Every time we perceive anything with our senses, the process of art has begun.

The second part of this process is the experience of an emotion because a sensory perception has been made. These feelings may be neutral, pleasant or unpleasant. They are still part of the process. At this point, the process of "art" has transferred information from one person to another. So, where art is concerned, there is always a transmitter and a receiver.

For example, the transmitter paints a picture and the receiver looks at it. Art happens when the receiver acquires some sensory impression from the picture that produces an emotion. The receiver "knows" in a very raw and elemental way some aspect of what the transmitter was offering. If I make a sculpture, paint a picture or write a poem, these actions may have therapeutic value for me, but the process does not become art until another person emotionally experiences some aspect of what I have created. Art is the process of transferring information between people in a way that circumvents the intellect.

Understanding is an intellectual process in which information is transferred. The process of understanding requires details, such as quantity, color, punctuation, logic and structure. Science is based on understanding. Understanding is the main process human beings use to transfer data.

Spirituality is based on knowledge. Knowledge is the innate recognition and emotional identification we experience through some level of perception. Art is the main process in which human beings transfer knowledge.

The first part of this book serves as record of my karma and my experiences in its transmutation. The first sixty-odd years were marked by my ignorance of karma and its restorative power. There was much loss, pain, and suffering, without much realization, knowledge, enlightenment, or healing.

In the second part of this book, representing the last five years or so, I have experienced the benefits of working with this process therapeutically and spiritually. In other words, the burning of my karma has allowed me to begin enjoying life again.

I am offering this to you, the reader, with the sincere hope that even a small portion of what is contained here may be of help to you. I encourage you to stop, observe, and decide to be a contrarian when it comes to your karma. Be an observer of your karma, and burn it every chance you get. Learn to respond to old negative patterns in new ways. Develop kindness, understanding and forgiveness for yourself and for those with whom you interact. Enjoy watching your sweater unravel, and be thrilled with who you find living underneath.

I do not write because I want to- I write because I have to. I have written these poems without any punctuation. I did this because my intention is to transfer the raw information and feelings that I have experienced with as little structure as possible. I try to write in packets. Sometimes these packets may have meaning for you, even as they stand alone. The lack of punctuation is intended to help you have multiple interpretations of this work that reflect your karma, not mine. This would be the most beautiful outcome for which I could hope.

THE KARMIC RIDDLE

Karma is considered by many to be a Universal Law. More specifically, a Universal Spiritual Law. Consider part of that term for a moment- Universal Law. There are many Universal Physical Laws that we all practice, believe or utilize. To name a few, there are laws of electrostatics, laws of motion, laws of thermodynamics and laws of gravity. These are laws that, to those who take the time to use them, make sense and provide a measure of peace of mind and predictability in the world around them. In other words, it makes them feel safe because part of the physical universe has become predictable.

The practice and use of these laws helps those who pursue further understanding of the physical universe to discover even more about the physical systems around them. It allows them to scientifically predict and develop hypotheses that may one day become new laws advancing human knowledge, understanding, safety and happiness.

In the realm of quantum mechanics, scientists would like to apply certain physical laws. However, they find they must interpret these laws somehow in order to get them to fit specific situations such as quantum gravity and quantum electronics. Does this mean that the scientifically-based physical laws that fit so well in the macroscopic world become arcane in the quantum world? It may only mean that the formerly cohesive physical laws are not completely applicable in the quantum realm because in this realm, new parameters must be taken into account.

And like quantum laws, spiritual laws must be first hypothesized and tested until distilled to an unimpeachable form.

Much of this work pertaining to understanding the spiritual realm has already been done for us. Thousands of years ago in India, sages, or master spiritual experimenters using methods of deduction and meditation, began delving into the mystery of consciousness. These men were not simply a group of people with nothing better to do. They were master observers, experimenters, and technicians who turned their attention inward in order to explore the basis of consciousness itself.

These men were no different than Isaac Newton, Albert Einstein or Nikola Tesla. The realm of consciousness, or spirituality if you prefer, is physically intangible. This is similar to what scientists have begun to experience along the outskirts of the quantum realm. When working on these levels, physicists including Einstein have utilized "thought experiments" in order to develop a hypothesis. This is no different than what the sages of ancient India did. They used the best techniques available that were applicable to the domain that they were studying.

Modern physicists are facing a new frontier. In the past, the physics of the outer world was the subject of scientific investigation. Now, physicists are facing a new frontier. There are new questions to be answered. Who is the observer, and how does the observer affect the quantum world?

Can our consciousness observe itself? And, where is our consciousness located? In the ancient Sanskrit hymns of the Vedas written thousands of years ago, Hindu investigators had already begun asking these questions.

I believe that it is shortsighted for science to assume that their well-practiced physical laws should be automatically applicable to other realms. Some believe that if these laws are not applicable, the realm does not exist. The quantum and spiritual realms are for the most part separate from the physical realm and therefore demand impartial scrutiny.

Karma is often referred to as the law of cause and effect. This is both understandable and practical. Karma does not take on a spiritual aspect until it is defined as the law of cause and effect throughout time and along multiple incarnations. It is not necessary to understand this aspect of karma in order to use this law to your advantage. All you need to know is that the concept of cause and effect has many parallels and goes by many names. We often hear sayings such as:
"What goes around comes around."
"One good turn deserves another."
"He/she will get what is coming to him/her."
"You will reap what you sow."

Take full advantage of your karma. Consider for a moment the mathematical and physical definition of the entity called a vector. In scientific systems, a vector is defined as an entity that contains magnitude and direction. Scientists use vectors to analyze and predict the effect of discreet forces on complex systems. The parallel here between science and the spiritual aspects of karma cannot be understated.

14

We can imagine that our karma is a spiritual vector. Karma includes the component of direction because it includes a sequence of events. Karma also includes magnitude because a sequence of events generates momentum. The complex system in this case is your life's journey.

There is another old adage which says, "I don't care if it is a law or not, it works for me, and I'm going to use it." One may say the same about gravity. I rarely think about it anymore, but I depend on it all the time. The spiritual aspect of karma is the part that makes it difficult for some people to understand or believe. This is because some people do not understand that we are all living in a spiritual realm as well as a physical realm. If this aspect bothers you, set it aside. You are alive now. You have a life to live now. The concept of cause and effect only needs to be understood within the context of your present life in order to be valid and useful.

Modern physicists have begun to observe the impact that perception or observation has on the quantum realm. In so-called "double-slit experiments" being conducted all over the world, photons, which are discreet particles of light, behave like particles under one condition and as waves under another. Remarkably, it is the presence of an observer that causes the photon to behave in one way or the other. Presence and observation are components of consciousness. If presence and observation in the quantum world can have such an effect, imagine how that effect may ripple out into the universe because we are all observers.

We live in an interactive, feeling and vibrational universe. One day we may realize that what we call the physical realm is nothing more than a manifestation of the spiritual realm. I believe that the quantum realm is the gateway to the spiritual realm. This is why scientific understanding begins to break down along the perimeters of the quantum realm, along the threshold.

Imagine that you are in the amusement park, the attractions are bright and loud, and you are holding your karmic pass in your hand. In addition to getting you here, your karma also suggests what to ride next. Unless you are addicted, it is just a suggestion. If you are addicted, it is a strong compelling suggestion; more of hook drawing you in. You always have choices, even if you are addicted. The choices just become harder to see.

If you are addicted, the best thing you can do right now is nothing, just for a moment. Choose to stop, turn around, and walk away from the next attraction if you can. Give your self a little time. Drive a wedge in it. Pause and realize that you have the power to make a choice, to check your karmic compass. Even if you cannot completely walk away, choose to walk a little more slowly. Make a conscious decision that you will just watch yourself and be curious about what you are feeling and thinking, then let go of it.

When you make the contrarian decision to react positively, even if not completely a reversal, you have begun burning your karma. When we start out with our first incarnation, or if you like, when we swing our feet out of bed in the morning, our karmic pass is full.

Our job is to burn all the karma on the pass, so we can return home to our source of contentment, peace and joy. Remember, where karma is concerned, you can only burn it or make more of it. You can never remain static for very long. Karma is a form of spiritual currency. It has no physical properties. It has no mass, no color, no shape, no spin and no flavor. Rather, it is the constantly changing summation on your spiritual balance sheet.

As I mentioned before, appreciation and gratitude are integral to this process. Kindness, forgiveness, generosity, empathy and gratitude are of great importance and have transformative power. I know it may be difficult to begin practicing some of these qualities, especially forgiveness. However, with enough practice you may actually get good at it. These qualities are the oil that lubricates the gears, shafts and wheels of the universe. Get out your oilcan, and be free with it.

Choosing to respond to challenges and people, particularly those who anger you or who have hurt you, with kindness and forgiveness can be very difficult. Learn to appreciate its difficulty, and slowly, over time, begin to revel in it.

Doing this type of work is not for the faint of heart. This is why the angels cry when they deliver a soul to become incarnate in a mother's womb. They know that the soul is being placed here to be tested, to do its work, and to burn its karma. Become a curious observer of your karma. Learn to identify with yourself as a spiritual warrior.

Become familiar with the terrain and learn to enjoy the benefits that come with living on the threshold. Know that as a spiritual warrior, you have access to levels of courage and strength beyond your current comprehension.

THE FIRST SIXTY YEARS

I have felt the pain of many losses. I have also had the benefit of much resolved or burnt karma. I have experienced the loss of children, family, friends, income, status and love. There were times when I was consumed with depression, anxiety, and desperation. My body was racked with stress, and I had become dis-regulated in almost every way. Then I found an anchor.

If you are hurting, and the pain has become so severe that you are suffering greatly, you must find an anchor. If you have been in pain for a long time and have become addicted, you must find an anchor. The use of an anchor serves to remind you and bring you back to some value, concept or quality that gives meaning to your life. Finding an anchor does not in itself burn karma. However it does quell the winds and storms around you long enough to light a match.

The most painful thing I have experienced was the loss of two of my children. After a second divorce and losing these children, their mother's onslaught of anger and destructiveness continued to impact the rest of my family and my career. I felt as though I was going to self-destruct. Very little happening in my life made any sense. I was depressed and anxious, and my finances and career were in ruin.

One morning, I was taking my two older sons from my first marriage back to their mother's house. We were in my old pickup truck headed towards the sun. The sunlight was streaming into the cab at a low angle. The light was shining on their faces and hands. Their skin seemed to glow like warm candle wax on Christmas morning.

Their hair was glistening with blond and auburn fire, and their blue eyes were radiant with light. I remember thinking, my God, what a gift I have been given here. In an instant I was struck by the irony, the bittersweet knowledge that I was losing two children while still blessed by the two boys in my truck.

At the time, I told myself that somehow I was going to anchor myself to these boys, and together we would live through this. I broke down and started crying with grief, joy and gratitude for what I had been given and for what I knew I was losing. I remember pulling the truck over because I could not see past my tears. My body had begun shuddering and convulsing as the emotions ran through me. My boys were frightened. They looked at me and asked what was wrong. I told them that I was okay and that everything was going to be fine.

Over the years I received several suggestions that I begin journaling. Great, I thought, as if it isn't bad enough to be living through this hell, now I have to write about it? Well, it seems writing has many benefits. It serves as a vent, a pressure relief valve of sorts for your emotions. It also helps to clear and organize your thoughts, and it helps you make emotional and spiritual connections. As I found out, it can be a powerful technique in burning karma. I began journaling, slowly at first, then actively, until I seemed to be writing all the time. I also did collage, sculpture and drawings as forms of art therapy. I remember sitting at the table, my heart broken from the loss of my two youngest children, and my life going nowhere. Holding a pencil, working with clay, or cutting a collage, I would begin to shudder, then sob and cry.

Then time would pass. I would look at the work in front of me, and like magic, a drawing, a sculpture or a collage would appear.

As I would reflect on my writing, reviewing my journals, I would often see a reoccurring theme. I was encouraged to write specifically on these topics. These themes and the writing became the flint and steel I needed to light the fire.

In the first part of this book, the poetry comes from the phase I call "The first sixty years" of my life. These years include all the major losses I have endured, including those of my childhood. In a karmic sense, the first sixty years of my life *are* my childhood, and it's resolution. I can now look back and see the same theme like a play that was repeated over and over with new karmic players, until I was cracked open, ripped apart, my heart scattered to the wind.

Most of the work in this section is undoubtedly contemplative and melancholy. This is so because the work served as a vent, a crucible, and a converter for my karma. In order to burn your karma, you must find a way to bring it out into the light and to liberate it from your soul. Become the alchemist to your karma. Experiment with different techniques. Begin transmuting your karma into immortality.

AS I SLEEP TONIGHT

She rings her hands in pain
Tears roll down her face
Lines cut her deep like acid rain
Her sobbing a disgrace

Her mind filled with the past
She moves from room to room
An inner peace that will not last
She prays within this tomb

Her hands filled with the future
As she stoops to do her work
A child now to nurture
Have I become the clerk

In the distance I sit quietly
Out of sight and mind
Forgiving her silently
For the fear that makes her blind

Day turns slowly into night
Moonlight washed away the sun
Out of mind and out of sight
I sit and wonder what I've done

She prepares the day's last meal
We pass the plates at hand
Everyone seated we make still
Pallbearers at the stand

The kitchen cleaned and beds are made
My brothers laugh and play
A last attempt at peace is staid
My heart in great dismay
Time for bed I cannot sleep

She sees that I have cried
She straightens her apron taps her feet
Her love she will provide

Like a Spanish galleon sailing
Many battles has she fought
Her rocking chair now wailing
It has become my cot

Safe among her rigging
Her sails push us out to sea
Toward a starry sky made spinning
My mistress makes her plea

I rest safely in your arms tonight
I feel your body next to mine
I rest safely in your arms tonight
An end to this salty brine

Her breast rises and falls in time now
Sobs come and go with lines made fast
Sleep ebbs and flows across her bow
On a ghost ship of the past

Together we cross a blackened sea
She's a slaver on the run
Arm in arm in poverty
Beating like a rowers drum

I rest safely in your arms tonight
I feel your body next to mine
I rest safely in your arms tonight
An end to this salty brine

CLOUDS

Storms build on the horizon
Racing toward the sun
Reaching ever upward they think of only one

Sunlight as their auburn hair
Nubile rounded forms
Reaching ever-upward nature's perfect storm

They bare their breasts and bellies
Linger stop and start
Reaching ever upward as worlds fly apart

Heaven's glory sets to shimmer
It's silent desperation
Reaching ever upward violet lips in exultation

Witness the sun's last tremor
As he does his best
Reaching ever upward his face turned toward the west

Content in their undoing
Shadows start to fade
Reaching ever upward heaven's tears of jade

With Vulcan's anvil ringing
The sky is split with light
Reaching ever upward a thousand birds take flight

At last a time for birthing
The wounded earth lies still
While reaching ever upward
Naked she takes her fill

THAT PERFECT DAY

How dare you
Why did you leave me when you did
How dare you
Why did you leave me the way you did

You are gone now
Some insignificant little fact has changed
A thing so small and yet the way the whole world
works has changed with it
A little part of me deep inside is lost and cold and
dark now
A little piece of hope that you once placed against my
heart to prop it up
Has come hopelessly undone

Why did you leave me on that... day
That bright beautiful sunny fall day
When the sky was like a big blue bowl turned upside
down
Fluffy white clouds and air so crisp and cool
Autumn swirling around my feet
The sun warm on my face and back
A beautiful day so full of promise so full of life
So full of you

I remember
I remember
It was a day when we tried to cheer each other up
Our false bravado catching like a splintered bone in
our throats
A day when I held your trembling hand like a bunch
of dried leaves
A hand that once was strong
A hand that guided me so many times before

That day I held your body close to mine and never
wanted to let go
A day when you held me
Close to you

I could feel your strength come and go
Leaving you breath by breath
Like the last throws of a once mighty locomotive
Life leaking out of you from little holes in your eyes
and ears and skin
Grain by grain like sand from a broken hourglass
Until your arms held me no more
Until it was only me left doing the holding
Until I knew there was nothing left for me to hold
Until it felt like the whole world had slipped between
my fingers
Falling falling falling away
Then I let go

I look at my life now
It is like a painting
A once beautiful scene
Brush stroke memories of blue green and gold
Expectations of love and friendship pink silver and
orange
The canvas now stained with smudges of grief guilt
tears and fear
On "that" day the canvas that was you and I was torn
in half
A ragged ripping sound
And now there is just this half
My half

Something has gone terribly wrong
Something that cannot be
Is
I thought I had prepared myself so well
I was sure that I was so much stronger than all of this
And yet
I was devastated

I tell myself I can go on without you
That it will take time and everything will be OK
That time heals all wounds
And that one day I will heal from all of this
But my heart says
Everything is not OK

I see your face in crowds of people
I crane my neck to get a better look
I hear your voice call out to me when I am alone
My heart skips a beat with anticipation
I smell the soap you used to bathe
And I know that you must be nearby

Then reality descends like a silent thunderbolt
The crushing weight of memory collides with the
brutality of logic
Smothering and suffocating me
The anguish that I had so skillfully buried
Erupts like an upturned grave
Spilling its contents in front of me
Forcing me to live through it all again

You are long gone now and I still feel anger
We were friends we were partners we were a team
Now you are gone and I am the one who is left here
all alone with all of this
I am the one who has to look in the mirror

I am the one who sees two black holes where his eyes
used to be
I am the one who cries out for you at night when the
house is filled with ghosts
I am the one who eats alone and is always hungry

There are days when I seem to function
When I talk and laugh and live again
Days when I look ahead and feel hope and promise
But there is never a day when I do not think of you
There will never be a day when I will forget you
There will never be a day when I will not miss you
There will never be a day when I will stop loving you

DOCTOR FEARMAN

As long as human beings exist
Society makes a place for me
I go by many names

To those that employ me I promote a sense of
comfort piety righteousness and political correctness

For those that must have an answer
I engender relief and confidence

For those that are brought to me
I instill fear pain anguish and loss
I create doubt and shatter lives

There are times I operate quietly and alone
Secretly doing what I do best
I make you talk
Spill the beans
Just you and me
Up close and personal
Eye-to-eye
Glove to skin
Mind to mind
In a bright antiseptic cold room

There are times when I work with others of my ilk
One specialist handing you over to another
Always professional and formal
Each of us with our wry little smiles
Which we give you with thin gaunt dry lips

You will tell me what I want to hear
What they want to hear you say
I am good at what I do
I write reports
I go to conferences
I enjoy seeing how you respond
How you all twist in the wind
As I turn down the screws

I have the approval of those in power
And that of my peers
They pay me well
I righteously go about my business
With the application of my craft
Condoned and justified
My family and friends respect me
I go to church
And the PTA

I have degrees and certificates on the wall
I am trained to be trusted
And justified by what I do

I have other things on the wall too
pieces of leather paper charts electrodes
and shiny cold sharp things
Things that encourage you to tell me what I want to
hear
Things we are sure are inside your head or body

Please tell me all I want to know
So I can send you along your way
Broken
I get paid well
And go home to my family
Safely

I work in dank and dirty places
And well-lit comfortable offices
My colleagues are spread across the earth

When the time is right
And the need is there
And reason gives way to fear
I spring up from the ashes of your broken dreams
From the shards of what is left of your life
I come from your trembling
Your screams and tears

I am convinced that I am good
That my services are needed
That I am within my rights
I roll up my sleeves
I pick up my tools
And begin again
Next

I AM NOW

Fears of the past are fading
I do not have to hide
I do not have to make myself small
I do not have to take small breaths
I do not have to be very still in the night
I do not have to freeze

I do not have to defend myself
I know who I am now
I know what I am now
I know why I am now
I know how I am now
I know where I am now

I cannot change what others think
I cannot change what others do
I cannot change the past

I make my choices now
I create my attitude now
I create my life right now

I am safe now
I can eat now
I can be myself now
I can feast now
I can breathe now
I can run with the wind now
I can pray now
I can relax now
I can sleep now
I can be with others now
I can be by myself now
I can dance now
I can laugh now

I can smile at a child now
I feel warm inside now
I can love now
I live in Grace now
I hear the voice of God now

I KNOW

During the dark stormy night
I know the dawn will come
I know the sun will shine

When my world is spinning out of control
I know that gravity will bring me to ground

When I feel sick
I know that health is my nature

When I feel confused
I know that all will become clear

When I feel weak
I know that strength is my birthright

When I doubt myself
I know that I will be successful

When I am alone
I know That Someone is always there for me

MY PERSONAL BILL OF RIGHTS

I have the right to ask for what I want
I have the right to say "no" to requests or demands
I have the right to express all of my feelings
I have the right to change my mind
I have the right to make mistakes and not be perfect
I have the right to follow my own standards
I have the right to determine my own priorities
I have the right to *not* be responsible for other people
I have the right to expect honesty from others
I have the right to be angry with someone I love
I have the right to be uniquely myself
I have the right to feel scared and say, "I am afraid"
I have the right to say, "I don't know"
I have the right to make decisions
I have the right to my own needs for space and time
I have the right to be playful and frivolous
I have the right to be healthier than those around me
I have the right to be in a non-abusive environment
I have the right to be happier than those around me
I have the right to make friends and be comfortable
I have the right to change and grow
I have the right to be treated with dignity and respect
I have the right to be happy

MY WHOLE LIFE

I have done everything to avoid the pain
the fear the loneliness anxiety and depression
I felt I was not worthy of being loved
In time I stopped loving myself
I assumed God did not love me either

A master of self-improvement cosmetic change and
positive thinking
None of this was working
Something more basic was not right
I sought a brother and confessor

Parts of me have died
Others are on life support

I must divest myself of layer upon layer
of rusted putrid armor

To look inside is to know pain
I dissect myself like a frog on a platter
I reel at the sheer impact of my misdirection
I unwind the self-taught story
And the barbed wire that encircles me

I must read the little stories out loud
The lies
And the ugly secrets that up till now
added up to me

My soul has been murdered
My heart fractured
My body violated

I must tear down the old life house

Sew the land with salt
Build a strong and true foundation

I desire to be naked in every way
To be totally vulnerable in every way
I must be distilled burnt away ravished
Until only my essence rises from the ashes
I let go of everything
I let go my goodness

I must find redemption and peace
I cannot do this alone

THE LEDGE

Out on a ledge
A hundred feet above the ground
Hands tied behind my back
A hot dry wind is gusting
Making little whistling sounds across my ears
Little whispers whimpers
Saying you are not strong enough

Just enough wind
To blow me over

My feet are bound together
I look down
It's not rope that binds me

They are hands
Twisted and knotted together like branches of a vine
Many hungry grasping hands
Clutching at my ankles
Twisting and gripping over each other
Like a nest of knotted snakes

Just a dream I say
As the wind makes me teeter back and forth
I lean back to keep from falling

How did I come to be here
Is this a dream
A nightmare
Someone else's nightmare

I sense someone or something standing behind me
Who are they
What do they want
Can they help me
Will they help me
I call out to them
The air reaches the top of my lungs
Reaches my vocal cords
A pitiful whimper escapes

As though I were gagged
Stifled by someone's suffocating hands
Wrapped around my neck

There are hands on my shoulders
And thumbs pressed into my neck
At last
Someone here to save me
To wake me

There is a dank dark coldness where I am touched
A chill runs from that point
Across my back
Down my spine
Pausing at my gut it grips me like a fist
Terror pouring down into my feet
Like cold cement
A chill so penetrating
I begin to shudder
A shudder I must quell
Stop it I think
Stop shuddering
The shaking will take me over the edge

I look down
People are there
Looking up at me
People I know
And some that I do not know
They seem not so far away
I can make out their faces
Looking up with their necks craned to one side
Slack jawed and hollow eyed
Waiting
Waiting for me to do something
Waiting for me to fall
Like a bowling pin
Teetering at the edge

Whoever
Whatever it is behind me
Slowly pushes me forward
I feel a cold damp corpse
Pressing against my back
No
I scream to myself
Stop
I will fall

That cold icy blue touch again
Skeletal and persistent

Slowly very slowly
I am pushed closer to the edge
Forward degree by degree
There is nothing I can do
I cannot yell
I cannot step back
I cannot resist the sweet sickening damp force
at my back
A force that promises an end to all this

I look up
The sky is reeling
More and more forward I tilt
Until I pass the balance point

The hands lift off my shoulders
I swallow my heart
I begin the first few degrees of falling
My gut wrenching
The only thing keeping me from going over
is my will not to fall
I scream out my innocence within the confines of my
skull
I plead for my life
For the lives of my children

I twist my neck and look over my shoulder
Who is doing this
Who would torture me this way
To my shock and dismay
I recognize them
All of them

They are blindfolded
Standing in a line
The first with her hands on my shoulders
Then the rest standing behind her
Each with their hands on the shoulders of the one
ahead
I know them

They play savior and executioner
Pushing forward
Then pulling back
As though it were some sort of macabre play
As though they do not know who I am
As though what they are doing was nothing personal

They hold me here
Suspended around a tipping point
Gently pushing me forward
Releasing me
Watching me fight for my life
Then pulling me back
Again and again
It seems to last a lifetime
I am frozen in terror and confusion

I would have nothing today
If I walked the earth
Free from those in this nightmare
Free from those who draw and spell
My karma

DIAMOND EYES

I move from branch to branch
While you stay very still
I feed upon the ground
While you look down until

I balance on the highest limb
As you look up at me
I sing a song to no one
While you sing out to sea

I fly away in fear
Your thoughts are far away
My song is melancholy
I never hear you say

I eat the sweetest fruits
You sip only the dew
I preen my golden feathers
As your trust returns anew

I am he with ruby eyes
That looks at you with anger
I am he with emerald heart
That feels the presence of a stranger

Who are you with empty eyes
To look at me in vain
Who are you with listless love
To feel so little pain

The moon and sun embrace
Rays of gold and silver tears
Your perch is vacant now
A prison through the years

I am always there
When you sing your song anew
I am always near
When you think your time is due

I am always at your side
When defeat is hardest won
I am always looking forward
When you bemoan a life undone

And when you look upon me
With eyes of crimson rage
Your mind obsidian with pain
As you dance upon life's stage

It is I who can truly see
With diamond eyes I gaze
I wrap myself around you
My amethyst heart ablaze

THE PASSAGE

We raise our eyes to heaven
Prayers not yet spoken
Offerings and subterfuge
Penance given as a token

Like the woven cloth around us
Time bends to warp and fill
While we lie here in our sleeping
Only moments left to kill

Gray winds pressing at the door
Time on the auction block
Apparitions one by one
Rattle at the lock

We each worship at the shrine
Fingers tremble round the clock
Grandeur glory penitents
We bow and then take stock

Warriors healers laborers
A siren's song is sung
Downy soft yet violent
A tender trap is sprung

Stronghold of the future
An open fortress of desire
A vault once held as sacred
At the crossroads of love and fire

It is at once all things
And nothing left as well
Introitus that envelops
A hohlraum sent from hell

Breech its velvet copper gates
Each story told anew
Weary legions yet to come
Emperors arrive askew

Runes cast with utter certainty
Her breath floats cross the glen
Sweet and sour salt and succor
We lie captive deep within

Pushing shouting mounting falling
Each times their deadly thrust
Slowly life is drained away
Victim to turgid lust

Battle won and war undone
Our senses are regained
Time passes slowly onward
Our tears turn into rain

Scintillating mind altering
Silver fills our sight
Whimpering and clamoring
Looked on with delight

The years are kind to some
Horrific loss to others
Sand slips through our fingers
As daughters turn to mothers

Slowly we are joined again
Driven by desire
Bested by our chemistry
Our minds echo liar liar

And yet it goes on and on
From cradle to the grave
Punishment and sweet reward
A hunger we cannot stave

ANTHOLOGY
SALVATION

Part One
The Quickening

How it all begins
A little glimmering
That little flutter deep in my chest
Somewhere way down inside
Below my lungs
The farthest recess of my heart
Back again into time and space
When there was only a black vast cold stillness
A universe waiting to be born

An infinite pinpoint of twinkling light
Velvety black that goes on and on through time
The silent glimmer stirs in me
My breath will fan this ghostly little light
Back and forth
Forth and back
Until the spark becomes a flicker
The flicker then a light
For moments I dwell here
A universe in the making

The slower I breathe the more slowly time passes
The last grains of sand
From an hour glass
Until it stops
The flicker now a flame it's the breath that carries me
Each inhalation a mighty pull at the oars
Each exhalation thrusts my little boat of
consciousness farther ahead

Across the gap of past and future that holds Men's
souls in limbo
Across the honey baited snares of love
And over the polished hooks of hate and revenge
Cautiously I move
Tentatively
Until

Across this void my nascent breath
The great abyss of thought and time and ego falls
away
To my left and to my right
The pillars of time
Creak and crumble
Split and shatter
Farther and farther I go
Leaving it all behind

My breath
The Prana of a million lost souls
Expanding and contracting all around within
As me
Until we are one breath

Deep and steady now
Like a child
Asleep in its mother's arms
An intergalactic rhythm
My mission
The firmament of my consciousness

On this vast plain of knowing
A single heartbeat gathers
A beat not unlike that which fills my veins
The beating of the field
A singularity
Here energy and information are one
The kindling of my passion
The quickening of my heart

Now comes the fire

ANTHOLOGY
SALVATION

Part Two
Fire

Fire is the pain that goes unspoken
Building and banking inside my head
It is the kindling of a blaze well made
A flame well stoked with thought
Crackling and hissing
That cannot be ignored
That holds the eye
That cannot be turned away from

It is the chalky creaking of my bones
The shock and tremor along my nerves
And the needles crawling under my skin

Now through my chest
And into my heart
It erupts like an angry anthill
A boil filled with
The retching heartbreak of loneliness
The bitterness of remorse
A ghostly boxcar of echoes and endless guilt
And the crushing black and blue of grief

It is a heat
A searing wall of pain
The alchemy of synapse and hormone
The ego's stilted flight from pain to suffering
A feverish incantation when I believe no one is
looking
A furrowed brow and sunken eyes when I believe that
someone is

The desperation of boundless loss
The memory of those who cannot be loved
Couched in the hollow faces and broken dreams of
those who will not be loved

Fanned by the illusions of a time bound mind
It is a smoking iron crucible
Glowing cherry red and orange
Boiling bubbling up
A heat so all consuming and complete
I must turn away from it
The very thought of it makes my mind shimmer
Like waves of heat rising from a forge
It becomes a specter of the suffering that is yet to
come
All the ego's contents are subjected to this reducing
flame

Fire is in the red and ochre of blood spattered
contracts
In the grays and gold of a daybreak
wrested from the blue cadaver's grip
A cold midnight dream
Of obsession and compulsion

This foreshadows a cooling of infatuation and hate
Seeming opposites which when examined more
closely
Melt and fold into one another
Shifting shape and meaning
Until all is lost to the confusion of comparison

At last at last
This is the vehicle of transmutation
The inner recess of my heart
An alchemist toiling deep within me
Witches the lead of time and suffering
Into the gold of present and peace

It is fire that lies at the threshold of understanding
That smoldering gap of creation

Truth knowledge change and enlightenment
With this conflagration I receive
The first glimmerings of inspiration
The first connotations of karmic sense
My caretaker when all else fails
The lynchpin of my beliefs

The roaring blaze is now condensed
A tiny violet flame
Inextinguishable in the raging storms
Of comparison fear and anxiety

If the eyes be windows to the soul
Then through fire
My hands and feet have become its wings

ANTHOLOGY
SALVATION

Part Three
Wings

Some of my memories come free and easy
Some are strung tightly together like knots along a
string
Place markers along the thread of time
The only ties I have with you

Am I a part of creation
Does the world still belong to me
At one time it did

Once upon a time it was enough
Your bright eyes and your little voices
Made the earth tip and spin for me

Now

My link with you is gone
My eyes no longer shine back to me in yours
There is only a shadow of myself
Starring at me from the past

My arms are tattered strips of gauze
My heart a weed filled vacant lot

Once I overflowed with your need for me
And your dreamy little sighs
My life was full

You were my babies
My children my life my world
You were my vision
My breath my blood my everything

What good are my feet
If they do not lead me back to you
What good are my hands
If I can not hold your little faces

What good is love
If your heart lies closed to me

A flight that beats and soars
From soul to soul we move
Until somewhere out there
We fall in love with humanity
And become God's fallen angels

What good are wings
If the angels all must fall
What good is my heart
If God is the only one left to love

We come to earth
As women and men
Stripped of our former glory
Fixated on a life
Filled with emotion pain and suffering

Never to return to heaven's canyons
And it's storied mountaintops
Never to sit at God's right hand
And see the folly of it all

The barter has been made
The contract drawn and quartered
My love for you is pledged
The deed is done and signed

My wings left far behind now
I seek a life with you
A life of hands and feet
A life of memories to keep

ANTHOLOGY
SALVATION

Part Four
The Prayer

Most of the time
Our lives are like a pencil and paper
Most of the time
We are merely what is written
We are what come after the fact
Most of the time our story
Is what is said and done
And it seems
There is nothing we can do about it

This prayer is for you
I am writing this prayer for us
I am writing this for the few
That feels there is nowhere left to go
No one to turn to
No ledge to place our feet

Most people have never been here
And I hope they never will
I feel gratitude and joy for them

But for the very few of us that have been
For the holiest of the holy that face this darkness
Alone
For those that can no longer bear
One more day of this
For those that feel that there only option
Is a sorrowful end
By their own hand
I write this prayer
This declaration of Self
This statement of power and freedom

My Beloved

Do you know what love is
Do you have an idea
Do you really know
Think on this now
As I prepare a place for you at my table

Do you know where love comes from
Or where it goes
When the object of your love
Has gone missing

Do you know where the love of God goes
That something you used to feel
Somewhere inside you
That little space of kindness
Deep in your heart
That is there no more

If I look at your face now I see only suffering
Wrinkles and creases
Put there by the most horrible of deeds
Deeds that you have done
Or that others have done to you

As I look into your eyes
Eyes that sting and burn
Because they have no more tears to give
I see the real you

As I look deeper
Deeper into your heart
I see a quiet cold hollow darkness
An endless pit
A deep cold well
Built from the stone and mortar
Of guilt and remorse
A dungeon made most dark
Bottomless
Where there is no light
No echo
A void so vast in its dimension of loss
That the tears you shed
Fall into it like virga
Never to reach the bottom

The pitiful sound of your wailing
Gives this ghostly place an address
A threshold and a form
That grabs you by the throat
And freezes you
Pinning you down tight
Like a sheet of plastic
That you can see through
But cannot breathe or speak through
Suffocating
The only sound you hear
The blood pulsing in your ears

This is a place most diabolical
It encases you in sorrow
And embalms you with suffering
This is a place hewn from
All the possibilities and promise
Your life holds no more
It all lies broken smoldering at your feet
This place is carved with rage
And chiseled deep with shame
The more often you come here
The more it draws you in
Until it is the only place you know
The only place left that welcomes you
A place you somehow understand
For all its morbid predictability
A hovel furnished with everything you desire
But can no longer touch
The longer you stay
The more sure of it you are

You are a point now
A small smudge of the pencil
On an open sheet of paper
No more than a dot
You have no height
No width
No length
And you are dying

How can you possibly survive
Much less thrive
Much less speak or breathe
Much less run or fight
Why would you want to

How can you rejoin the living
The world
Society
When so much that defines you has been lost
Or taken from you
Or worse yet
Given up by you

Your children
Your home
Your health
Your spouse
Your savings
Your career
Your self-respect
Your position in the community
Your friends

Indeed
Your innocence

As you look at the paper in front of you
The dot is the story that is written
The paper is the Field of Infinite Possibility
The pencil your hands feet and voice
As you look at this caricature of yourself
Tears begin to flow
They fall like yellow drops of acid
Raising little blisters
On your hands and the paper below

Pause now my friend

Take a moment and just breathe
Feel your chest expand
And feel your body settle down
As you exhale

Muster any scraps of courage you have left
And let your breath clear your tortured mind

What you choose to do next
Means the difference between life and death
Between tomorrow and the end of days

I place my arm around you
I put the pencil in your hand
I can feel you sobbing
Shuddering

We look into each other's eyes
And for the first time you see who you truly are
Reflected back in mine
You see the first person that truly understands
Who truly knows your pain

You begin to sense
There may be a chance
Because someone else has survived this
Someone else has come out alive
Maybe just maybe
You can make it out too

For the first time in a very long time
You feel a glimmering
A slight possibility
Like the strange scent of spring
Somehow carried on a winter breeze
You have a choice
Now
In this very moment

Take it

Against everything you have known and felt for a very
long time
Against all that has been black and dead and decaying
There is a ray of light

You sense that there is some part of you
That is still pure and whole and complete
Perfect
And incredibly very powerful

You start where you are
You put the tip of the pencil on the single point
The point that has been you for so long

And you push it

Something stirs within you
Your fingers keep on pushing
Your life is a line now
You have length now
You can see a beginning
And a path forward
And as long as you keep the pencil moving
You have a chance
You have a future

You can feel yourself breathing
You are conscious of your arms and your legs
Your hands and your feet
You can speak your truth
You are alive
You are free to live another day

I can tell you my friend
This will not be easy

How does one begin again from ruin
Without all the beliefs
The people
And the things
You used to love
And that used to love you

You will do what our kind has always done
You will fan the flame
You will reinvent
And reconstruct yourself
You will find new people and places and things to
love
You will learn to burn your karma
Your mind and your body will heal
And be refreshed

One day
You will look in the mirror
And for the first time you will see
A beautiful and infinitely powerful version of yourself
Your True Self
Looking back at you
Eyes filled with love and self-acceptance
And you will come to know the gift of karma

I LET YOU GO

Once you were my constant friend new and secret
You protected me
Then old and tested you slayed me
I once held you to my breast while the fires and
quakes of my parent's tirades battered me
Then I held you at arm's length as you amazed and
dazzled me
And finally you ravished me with a fury I could not
understand
You became a secret and horrible weapon I could use
And that was used against me
Then you became another me
And then the only me

You are not my friend any longer
You are not my enemy
You are not on my skin any longer
You are not in my gut
You are not in my brain any longer
You are not in my veins
You are not behind my eyes any longer
You no longer hang on the wind like my breath in
winter
You make me freeze no more

I see your tortured contorted face now
I smell your acrid breath
I feel your deep blue cold now
I touch your scaly hide
I taste your bile on the back of my tongue
I sense all of you and know
That you are no longer who I am

I release your tortured soul
I give you back
I let you go
I release you to the religion
That condemned and doubted me
I release you to those that sought to change and slay
me
I release you to the lawyers
That tortured me with promise and impoverished me
I release you to the judges
That took my children from me
I release you to the doctors and western medicine
That humiliated and dissected me
I release you to the police
That processed me
I release you to the government
That ridiculed and stripped me
I release you to the corporation
That addicted and shackled me
I release you all those that fear me
As I have feared you
I release you to the wind
I release you to the universe
I release you to your cold dark heart

I am not afraid to feel the pain
I am not afraid to be cold
I am not afraid to walk alone
I am not afraid to be who I am
I am not afraid to sit with hunger
I am not afraid to be loved
I am not afraid to love
I am not afraid to be hated
I am not afraid to breathe
I am not afraid to say what I believe
I am not afraid to say that I have known you
I am not afraid to be with you

I am not afraid to hold you
I am not afraid to comfort you
I am not afraid to sleep with you

This is my present right now
This is my life right now
I let you go

THE NEXT 30 YEARS

The second part of this book begins about five years ago when I turned sixty. Most of the major spiritual and emotional issues I had been tasked with through my karma were resolved. The poems in this section reflect a less melancholy and a more optimistic outlook.

COME WITH ME

Come walk with me
Kick off your shoes
Take my hand
Be neither here nor there
But somewhere in between

The crossroads of past and future
The creeping ochre edge of darkness
Meets the crimson hem of dawn
Pause here for an instant

Between thoughts
Between breaths
And lives

Our hearts
Hang like paintings
In the hallways of endless time

Trace this jagged line of light
Along a volcanic rift
Across a no-man's land of darkness
Skip along its gilded path
Here one moment
Gone the next
Time and place
A memory
A discarded map of long ago

The sea rolls gently to the shore
Sky blue washes over our feet
Then orange red and lavender
A watercolor forgotten in the rain

A solitary momentary place
Of serf sand and sun
Of solid liquid vapor light
A home to wraiths and sprites

The morning sun kisses the shoreline
A promise of warmth and light
The tide gives birth to foam and mist
And creatures of the deep

This is a place of prayer
Moonlight ragas
And infinite possibility
A furtive dance of flute and santoor

Here is freedom from time and space
Where silent contemplation
Leads to an emptiness of mind
And a lightness of being

Thoughts give way
Synchronous indigo harmonic waves
Everything you have learned
Becomes a burden
Left gladly on the roadside
A trap for scheming fools

The more that you release
The faster you are propelled into the abyss
With no judgment or attachment

Observation and awareness
All contained within you
Placed there for your journey
You hold to none of it

No easy or difficult here
No happy or sad
Good or bad
Only abandonment of mind
Expansion of self
Of presence
Contemplation
And rapture with the Devine

DREAMSCAPE

The world is filled with much to see
And much I turn away from
So much once seen
Becomes so much of what I fear
And so much then avoided
A framework of what I would become

What holds my gaze today
What little thing do I see clearly
So vividly
So plainly
That I invite it into my bed like a lover
Like the pillow beneath my head
Careful not to crease it
I smooth my hands across it
I hold it close to me
My heart a shield for it
As much as it shields me

I say a prayer of absolution
Beg forgiveness for myself
My mind falls deeper and deeper into it

I am carried off to sleepy fields
Of waving golden wheat
Covered by tepid lavender skies
Spotted with billowing spinnaker clouds
Floating in the breeze

Daytime visions melt
Surreal images of good bad and the absurd
Like Crayons on a summer sidewalk
Enfolding into and onto themselves
Over and over and over again

The kaleidoscope of my mind
Images lilt and dance
Mend and rend
And mend themselves again

Needles made from silver shafts of light
Pulling threads spun from a unicorn's mane
Off I go sewn into the stuff of dreams
The land of never ever more

Grey smoky mists of spring
Curl like little dancing pearls
Pulsing threads along the spider's web
A shimmering mirage of wind blown dust
A black ribbon of hot desert highway
Fading in and out and into sight again
Teasing my eyes as I rub them clear once more

My newborn's furtive gaze
Fixed on me for the first time
My childhood flashes across his periwinkle eyes
Flickering scenes from an old newsreel

Now snowflakes big and fluffy
Floating suspended on my steaming breath
Land upon my nose
And melt into droplets of milky melon dew

Old tattered dusty books fall open
Worn wrinkled memories
Yellowed snapshots
A day in the life of my ancestors
Old and young alike
Held hostage on the page
Stare back at me
With hollow wooden eyes
From a prison called the past

Lives once full of expectation
All of them are gone
Even the children
Even the babies
Even their dreams

When does what I see
Become an aspect of what I am
When does being seen
Become that which defines me

Is it more important that I see
Or that I be seen
Seeing and being seen
Spiritual dialogue between lost souls

Do I see
Do I dream
Has looking become a dream
And dreaming become
Living
Breathing
Revelation
Redemption

I rub my face open my eyes
Wince and curse the dawn
Sunlight falls into my pupils
Like cold water running down a rusty drain

Where does the light go
Has my light
Become
Your light
Your vision
Your dream

Our destination

AUTUMNAL EQUINOX

Slanted beams of sunlight
Make their way like spiders along the wall
Down and farther down
Into dusty corners of the room
Pushing the darkness away
Prodding
Slowly convincing afternoon's stubborn grey shadows
To run ahead along the floor

With each day that comes to light
That winks in and out of mind and soul
And goes away again at dusk
We inch farther from the light
Closer to the night
Cooler highs and lows

Father Sun grows tired now
His best work done in June July and August
Raising crops of standing wheat
Stirred by the wind
Flowing like liquid golden light
Stalks heavy
Pregnant with seed
They bow their heads
And await the farmer's scythe

Standing groves of trees
Their longing trunks with branches reaching
Push higher and higher still
Into a sapphire dome of afternoon sky
They strain against their roots
Like gypsy moths
Spiraling ever upward
To reach the object of their affection

The once mighty beast of fusion and light
Who fueled summer storms and hurricanes
And propelled vast columns of dust
For miles across the Sahara
Is now in decline
More pleasant than polite
His warmth a fleeting footnote
To the crisp cool air of fall

Even at midday
He works on bended knee
His back bent and stooped
He turns his attention away from us
And to his long lost brother
Proxima Centauri

His once powerful stinging rays
Of silver-white and iridescent platinum
Have cooled
Mellowed and recoiled
A serpent's final strike

His light
Now the yellow gold and orange
Of late summer narcissus
His blazing beard of halo and fire
Has become an orange solar flare
Tangled and looped
Great heaping dreadlocks
Around his wizened face

Now it is Father Sun that sweats and toils
To do his daily chore
Peasants gleaning in the fields
A corona of late season heat
Tears of gold
The disguise he wears
Memories of his brilliant glory

Now it is time for Mother Moon
To rule the heavens
And the midnight sky
To light the harvest fields
And bring meaning
To creatures of the night
She tugs at our emotions
As we swoon and dream
In our sweat soaked fallow beds

Her body floats seductively
A naked silver silhouette
Her light a pearl handled switchblade
Cleaves the darkened fields
Gossamer tendrils of the Milky Way enrobe her
A passing nod to modesty

In all her nocturnal splendor
This cool seductive orb
Shimmers in our eyes and hearts
A mayfly
Floating past a candle's light

Her sated beauty fills the heavens
Mocks the light of day
Makes a compact with the Devil
And with a final whisper
Seals the night away

INSPIRATION

Fire change truth and knowledge
A cauldron hewn of bleached and chalky bone
The violet light of things once cherished
Now burnt
Rising to my nostrils
The smoke of pride and fury
Pungent incense
The sweetness of anticipation
Spirals through time and memory
Ghosts of envy
Sprites of anger
The specter of yet another loss
And yet another victory

Hammers fall on tattered copper armor
Clanging ringing
Pealing inside from ear to ear

Fades away

The periphery of consciousness

Mighty imagination fails
The fear of knowing blends
With the doubt of understanding
Shades of amber viscous flowing
Sticky liquid oozing time
Sparkling shards of future lying on the floor

Collisions of past and present
The transmutation of righteous passion
Fear to hatred becomes anger
Then acceptance
Then love to selfless peace
Inspiration carried on the heavy breath of insight
Come visit me once more

PRANA BREATH

I breathe in
I breathe out
Air moving past my lips
Over my tongue down my throat
Lungs filling with air
My chest expands
My belly moves outward

The inward breath expands
Until it stops
Everything comes to an end
The earth frozen on its axis
My heart stops
Time stops

The universe shudders
The earth shifts and lunges forward
Air moves out of my lungs
My chest begins to fall
Air moves past my throat
Cascading over my tongue and lips
Spilling crashing out of me
Like a tidal wave
A tsunami of past and future

I am not breathing
I am breathed
I am a thread in the fabric of time
Cosmic flotsam blown across the universe
A living piece of space-time
A smoky wisp of being
A fleeting bit of memory

Prana all around me
Everywhere
In me
As me
Through me
The breath of countless millions gone before me
It does not stop within me
It surges through my body
Like an arc from cell to cell

Prana stokes the little violet flame that is my soul
Fans it back and forth until
Raging light and heat consume me
Tangents vectors lanes of flashing violet and gold

I am part of everything that is
Atoms fibers tendons stars
I am the instant of creation
The cauldron of the sun

A cold dark singularity
Sparked into endless light and heat
A memory of a memory
An eternity of the Now

Tumbling rolling lightning struck
Time booms across the void
From supernova to synapse
A never-ending ebb and flow
A shadow's dance of light
Every cell molecule and fluid
Knowledge light and love
Pulsing breathing gathering flowing
Like an electrical storm along my veins

Twisting my body
The endless breath of breaths
Like a pack of hungry wolves
Howling out my name

Swirling souls gather all around me
Spinning pulsing in and out of me
The vortex pulls me upward
My feet have left the ground
My heart is now expanding
Pushing higher and higher
A Dervish of thunder and lightning

Until the earth
This precious little stone
Spins ever more slowly down
Far far below
Stars and galaxies dance all around
My soul remains the witness
My eyes no longer see
There is no division
Only heart and breath for me

INTRICATE

It's not simple and it's not easy
It's intricate
One piece fitting into another piece
Then another and another
It's complicated
It's precise
A puzzle
It's intricate
Snick snick gears enmeshed with each other
Part of the whole
Necessary to the process
It's intricate
Slipping rolling sliding
Bearings move on shafts
Levers pulleys gears nuts and bolts
Turn to
Ratchet up
And gear down

People talking people working people walking
People loving
People pulling apart
This is intricate
We are intricate parts of the Universe
We are an intricate part of all that is
I am an intricate part of you
And you of me
Little wheels spinning round and round
Clicking whirring tumbling
Each gear synchronized with the little wheel next to it
Round and round we go
Spinning out into infinity

Where does it all stop
We are connected to the whole
And at the same time
Complete unto ourselves
Indivisible inseparable irresistible integral irrefutable
Intricate

SILENCE

What is it that it is not

Silence

A gap between breaths
The reflection at the end of a sentence
A moment left untouched by thought
An expectation at days end
A pause between lifetimes

Silence is the stock in trade of meditation
It is the currency of the Divine
The road to abundance is paved with it
It is the fertile garden of all that is desired

Silence is all that is
All that is needed
And all that is expected

Silence is left behind in our mother's wombs
Discarded like a broken toy when we were children
Used as a weapon by adults
Abhorred by our survivors when we die

We all return to silence
The thing we all search for
Without knowing it is missing

There are many substitutes but no replacements
We are convinced that it has no purpose and no value

It is silence that brings us to our knees
We turn away from it when it is exactly what we need
We fill the gap with our addictions
All our protestations
All the noise

Silence is our first and only home
It allows our hearts to beat
It stills our minds
And heals our bitter words

It surrounds the still small voice

THE GATEWAY

Who is this little child that waits for me
This little one who sees right through me

Past the gates through the bars
Off in the distance lies the city
Bright and sparkling in pink and emerald green
Beckoning to me like the Land of Oz
The specter of wealth and riches
Sears my eyes and starts my mind
Runs along my optic nerves
Crashing into the back of my skull
Like a freight car filled with fleeting dreams

Who is this baby that waits for me
This little one that sees right through me
The one with clean and mismatched clothes
The one with stormy marble eyes

I stand here my face pressed against the bars
Bars that sweat and tremble in my hands
From the effort of keeping it all in
I see the city I hear the music
It beckons from far far away

Boom boom boom boom
Rat a tat tat tat tat
Boom boom boom boom
Rat a tat tat tat tat

It is the promise of all things delicious
An invitation of excitement love and happiness
The sirens song of hope
And the banshee's cry from hell

Who is this little one that waits for me
At the crossroads of here and now
This little girl that sees right through me
The one with clean and mismatched clothes
Standing here on wobbly legs
Holding out her little hand

I pass this way each day
Shining spires out beyond the bars
The sound of the marching band

Boom boom boom boom
Rat a tat tat tat tat

The sound of wealth
The scent of riches on the wind
Curling up my nose and ears like barbed wire
Shiny black twitching earwig beetles
Boring bloody holes in my brain

Boom boom boom boom
Rat a tat tat tat tat

Who is this little one that waits for me
At the broken gates of hell
This little girl that sees right through me
With clean and mismatched clothes
Teetering on her little legs
Holding out her little starfish hand to me

This time I stop and look at her
Her expression blank
She tilts her head
I realize that she is blind
The orbits of her eyes like swirling clouds
On a cold grey winter sky
Swirls of stormy liquid pearl
No pupils
No little black holes to let in the light
No little black holes to let in the world
Yet she sees right through me

This fence is broad and huge
Thick cold twisted black bars of steel
Erupt from the ground
Extend up into the clouds
And out along the glen as far as the eye can see
A fence of twisted blackness
Hot forged and hammered by Lucifer's own hand
In the dark and smoky mists of past and future mind

What is this place
What is the prize within
This drusy gem
That is so valuable
So desirable
So attractive
So precious
That it must be protected
With a hellish fence like this
And yet its massive gates lie open
Rusted to the hinge

And this little girl is here

I stop again and look at her
As she tilts her head toward me
I know that she is blind
And yet she sees right through me

Her opaque gaze galvanizes me
Stuns me
Rivets my feet to the ground
And at the same time fills me with a peace
A freedom I have never known

My heart goes out to her
In her vulnerability
Her blindness
And I say to her
Hello little one
Why are you here
She holds out her pink little starfish hand to me
Turns her head
And suddenly I know that she is deaf

Yet she knows that I am here
And we both understand
That there is something primal
Something powerful
Electric
Mystical
Sacred
Something that words can only diminish
Binding us together

I am frozen where I stand
Who is this little waif
This little ragamuffin
Who is blind and deaf
Who sees and hears me move
Who knows of and all about me

Not knowing what else to do
I choose to take her hand

She smiles at me
She smiles for me
She smiles into me
Just for me and no one else
A smile as radiant and warm as sunshine
My heart is filled with glorious golden light
Filled with safety
Filled with peace
It soars and expands
In greater and greater circles
Until is seems it will explode

Then I catch my breath
I breathe

The same breath she is taking
The same air
The same Prana
And I am with her once again
Present here and now

I look across the gateway
The city recedes into the haze
The music a dull and distant thrum

I know that all the power and purpose
I will ever need is right here
Right now
In my hand

Every morning I walk to the gateway
Every morning little Purusha waits for me
Every morning I have a choice

LOVE IS A RIVER

Love is a pool of clear cool water
Sleeping in our hearts
Whispering when we are quiet
Singing like a lark

Soothing us in sorrow
Smooth as glass and dew
Like a mountain lake
Powerful and blue

It falls like gentle rain
Richness of the soul
When we have a thirst for it
It will take a toll

It is surely welcomed
As hearts begin to stir
Given never taken
Our ego's saboteur

IT'S A FACT

Dear man or woman
It's a fact
There are twenty-four hours in the day

Dear friend
It's a fact
There are sixty minutes in the hour

Dear lover
It's a fact
There are sixty seconds in a minute

My Beloved
It's a fact
There is an eternity
In the present moment

I am with you forever

STEEL BLUE

For: Patricia Miller

Long lost photos
Fill vacant jigsaw spaces on the wall
Memories
Stories
Laughter and tears
Somehow it all pulls together

Feelings of pride
Remorse
Guilt
Sorrow
Shame
And anger

You were a child
Then a little girl
Beautiful
Magical
Trusting
Loving
And innocent

Your infant eyes of blue
Glistening beautiful eyes
That strange shade of twilight
Before the sun makes its way into darkness
Showing us both the good and the bad
And all of the in between

You were placed here to live and thrive
With no promises or excuses
Like the rest of us
Placed here to experience life
To have your heart broken
Your life shattered
Then re-shaped and re-molded
Heated and hammered out
In God's own forge

As you grew
Your trust and heart were tested
Then rent in half
Like a lightning bolt splits the sky
Into day and night
Light and dark at the same time

Stunned and confused
How could this be happening
How can I protect myself
And defend myself
Where is my father
My mother
Anyone to protect me

The world changed for you that day
And slowly changed how your eyes see

Your brow
Your face
The muscles around your mouth
That magical place that used to be so quick to smile
And make others smile and laugh
Was gone
And then gone again

You are a woman now
Your eyes fully open to the world
No longer a child's eyes
They are a cooler thinner
More atmospheric shade of blue

They are eyes of hammered steel
Tempered and polished by the fires of loss
And the pain that comes from a story
That cannot be told enough

You are no longer so quick to accept
The world and its ways
Stories of victims and victors
Or fairy tale princes and princesses

You now have the eyes of the Osprey
Practiced in the dance of the hunter
And the hunted
They are the eyes of one who now commands
The riches of earth
The stormy skies above
And the roiling sea below

These eyes are made of polished steel and sapphire
Accustomed to the vagaries
And misfortunes of life
You are a spiritual warrior
Your shield
Your eyes and wings
Your sword
Your beak and talons

Within you
The pure heart of the child still sings
The fairytale song
The same heart
In the photographs

Within you
That loving baby smile
Still glows like an ember warming your heart
The same smile
In the photographs

The power of innocence and vulnerability
Is your birthright
No one can take it from you
You can only give it away
This power
Lives and stirs within you
Shining forth as strength and forgiveness
A beacon to light your way

This power comes from a holy sacred place
Your spiritual vault and tabernacle
Protected by you
And which in turn protects you

There is calm peace and safety here
And from this place
You are free
To spread your wings and soar
And live your life anew

PERMISSION

It is the loftiest and most audacious action
We can all aspire to
Before it lays the smoldering ruins of all your
protestations
The tears and broken dreams
Of all your half hearted attempts
And dire misdirection

It is the most misunderstood
The most effervescent
Benign
Gentle
Most elusive
And most powerful force in the universe

It is the distillation of all spiritual work
The most precious whispered secret
From human mind to human heart
A sacred covenant that only we can author
The most blood stained contract we will ever sign
The highest and most fortified of all our vanities
The most shameless act of will ever attempted
A fortress built of pain grief and guilt
Transmuted at once to power and peace

Below it lies all of Man's thoughts and computations
All of our passions and desires
All our hopes that we call transcendent

Forgiveness
Love
Grace
Enlightenment
Salvation
Redemption

These are the handmaidens of the Spirit
All must cede their power
Must wait their turn
Must do their bidding
Must genuflect and acknowledge
The grandest
Most refined
Sublime
And esoteric quality of all

It is looking in the mirror
Thousands of times
Over thousands of years
And seeing only loss imperfection and what is broken

One day

You notice something more
And for the first time
Your Spirit's eyes look back at you
With love and acceptance

You are whole
You are unleashed
You are permitted

You become accustomed to the sight
Accustomed to the feeling

And you long for this

And your heart breaks for this

Looking at your true Self
You see the Grail
In the deepest most unassailable chamber of your
heart
The Tabernacle

And you feel God is here
And you know that everything is Sacred

THE WIND

The wind makes no sound
How could it
The breath is quiet too
This how the story is told

Wind moves across the earth
Silently
As breath moves from the lungs
Silently

Obstruction cleaves the air
And gives rise to sound

Only when channeled does the breath
Give rise to voice
Speaking the story of the heart and body
The karma of the soul

Without the movement of wind over rocks and trees
The earth has no voice

Without the movement of breath from the body
Our fears remain locked in the flesh

Can we sing without the breath
Can the trees dance without the wind

Can we whisper love without the heart
Can nature tell its story without the sun

All forms of spirit return to God

Carried on the wind
Carried on the breath

MASKS

Who is that looking back at me
The mirror does not lie
Who is that looking inside out
The self I must untie

Must I always be looking
Or is it time for me to see
Must I always be comparing
Or is it time for me to be

Like shadows melting into darkens
Like daylight dripping from the sun
Who I am and whom you see
Are you and I the one

A story of I'm not good enough
So I must lie about who I am
A story of I'm not worthy enough
Until I become the lamb

When I look into the mirror
The mirror does not lie
It is I who tells the story
Of an ego that will not die

THE WALL

You are known as Mountain
Rock
Gym
Or Pitch
Some call you Boulder
Route
Problem
Or the Virgin the Young Woman and the Monk

Did I come here today to stand before you
As your equal
Or are you here today to stand before me
As my teacher
My master
I am a beginner once more
Teach me that which I already know
But have long forgotten

You are tall
You are cold
You are an abyss of silence and presence

I am small
I am sweating
Unsure of my next move

I know that there is work here
Work that must be done
Work for my bones muscles mind and spirit

My head is filled with voices
Some say you can do this
Take the first step
Other say leave now walk away
While you still can walk

No one will know if I leave
No one except you and I

This place is a shrine
Sacred ground
Many come here to worship
I stand before you and place my ego at your feet
It is the only piece of gear I will not need today

Have I come to you
Or have you come to me

Do I need you
Or do you need me

I take a deep breath and look you over
My eyes flicker from hold to hold
Up and down
Right and left
My mouth is dry
There is a lump in my throat when I swallow
I pour my senses over you
I can taste you
And smell you on the air

There seems no end to your mysteries
Your power
Your resolve
Your timelessness
No end to the stories that you tell
No end to the pathways chiseled into your face
That craggy personality of yours
And your hulking mass
Like a muscled juggernaut
Come to rest

I touch you gently
And you begin to stir
Your heart begins to beat
You shift and rumble and say
Go away little man
Take your shinny little toys
And your funny shoes
And walk away
For you annoy me
I am tired from carrying all this weight
For all this time
And I must sleep

There is an ancient intelligence at work here
A power deep inside
A geologic fairy tale
Passed down from crystal boundary to inclusion
Through eons of time
Stories of lightning
Thunder
Sunlight
Glaciers
Rain and snow
And the restless force of gravity
That brings us all to our knees
Even you

It is a story told among the trees
And mountains
The rivers
And the sky

It is this wall that calls to me

KIN

Every man is my brother
My father my son and then
Every woman my sister
My mother my daughter my kin

Every child is lost to me
Until they all come home to keep
Every joy and sorrow
Rejoins me as I weep

I am all things to everyone
Everyone means all things to me
Our parents say they love us
But give us unto death's tree

You are the sweetest thing
My grandmother my grandfather my friend
The shadow of my wings
The descendants and ancestors I defend

Is it faith that faith abounds
Or reason that saves the day
We live our lives in treachery
Lest Lord Yama have his way

Dear Reader, it is with a great sense of completion that I offer this work to you. A page from my book of life has been turned. You have my respect for who you are and for everything you have accomplished in your life. It is my sincere hope that we will meet one day on the karmic planes of Kurukshetra.